WIT

# Whose Skin Is This?

## A Look at Animal Skin—Scaly, Furry, and Prickly

Written by Lisa Morris Kee
Illustrated by Ken Landmark

Content Advisor: Julie Dunlap, Ph.D.
Reading Advisor: Lauren A. Liang, M.A.
Literacy Education, University of Minnesota
Minneapolis, Minnesota

Whose Is It?

PICTURE WINDOW BOOKS
Minneapolis, Minnesota

For Charlie Kee, my great boy—L.M.K.

Editor: Nadia Higgins
Designer: Melissa Voda
Page production: The Design Lab
The illustrations in this book were prepared digitally.

Printed in the United States of America.
1 2 3 4 5 6 08 07 06 05 04 03

**Library of Congress Cataloging-in-Publication Data**
Kee, Lisa Morris, 1962-
  Whose skin is this? : a look at animal skin—scaly, furry, and prickly / written by Lisa Morris Kee; illustrated by Ken Landmark.
    p. cm.
  Summary: An introduction to the various kinds of skin and skin coverings that animals have.
  ISBN 1-4048-0010-7 (lib. bdg.)
  1.  Skin—Juvenile literature. [1. Skin. 2. Body covering (Anatomy)
  3. Animal defenses.]  I. Landmark, Ken, ill. II. Title.
  QL941 .K34 2003
  591.47—dc21          2002007319

Picture Window Books
5115 Excelsior Boulevard
Suite 232
Minneapolis, MN 55416
1-877-845-8392
www.picturewindowbooks.com

# Do you have the itch to find who's who?

Look closely at an animal's skin. Skin can look shiny, prickly, or bumpy. Skin can be as hard as bone or as soft as tissue paper. Some skin is covered with fluffy feathers. Some skin is covered with thick fur.

Skin can tell you how an animal hides from its enemies or how it stays warm. Skin can fool you, too. Skin that looks smooth might suddenly be covered with prickly spines!

Animal skins don't all look alike, because they don't all work alike.

Can you tell whose skin is whose?

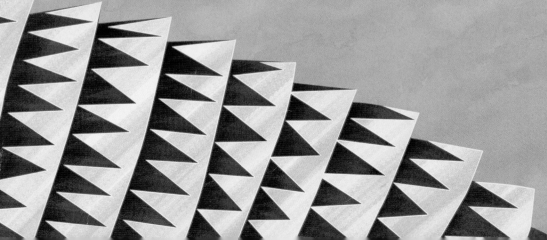

Look in the back for more fun facts about skin.

3

Whose skin is this, so smooth and bright?

4

5

This is a poison frog's skin.

This frog's skin is coated with a deadly poison. The bright color of the skin is a warning: "Don't eat me!" Even a tiny taste can kill a lizard or a monkey.

Fun fact: Poison frogs are colored to make other animals notice them. The frog's skin oozes poison, making it dangerous for another animal to even touch it.

Whose skin is this, so puffed and prickly?

This is a porcupine fish's skin.

A porcupine fish usually keeps its spines pressed flat against its skin. If a bigger fish gets too close, the porcupine fish sucks in water and puffs up into a big, prickly ball. The bigger fish swims away to find something easier to eat.

Fun fact: When a porcupine fish is puffed up, it can't swim away. It just bobs along like a balloon.

Whose skin is this, covered in shiny fur?

This is a sea otter's skin.

Water slides easily off the otter's oily fur.
The thick fur keeps the otter warm, even in
the freezing ocean. The fur traps the
otter's body heat next to its skin.

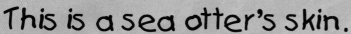

Fun fact: An otter has extra
skin between its back toes.
The webbed feet push through
the water like flippers, helping
the otter catch food and
outswim its enemies.

10

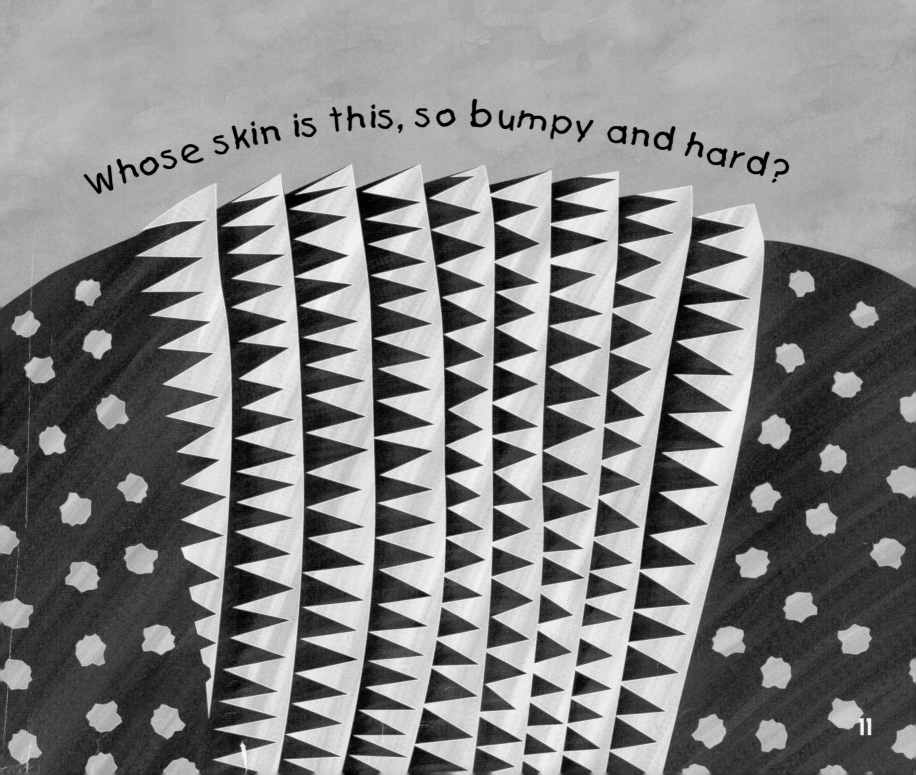

Whose skin is this, so bumpy and hard?

This is an armadillo's skin.

An armadillo's skin is made of hard plates that protect against thorns and brambles. A nine-banded armadillo often digs its den near prickly bushes. When attacked, it can run easily under the bushes while its enemy gets stuck behind.

Fun fact: When a three-banded armadillo is in danger, it curls up into a hard ball. The tiny pink fairy armadillo runs to its den and blocks the opening with its hard, scaly rear end.

Whose skin is this, flashing a warning?

This is a coral snake's skin.

A coral snake's bright stripes warn other animals that its bite is poisonous.

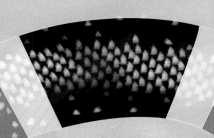

coral snake

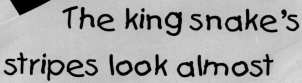

Fun fact: Both the coral snake and the king snake have red, yellow, and black stripes, but their stripes are in a different order. A rhyme helps us remember which snake is poisonous. It goes, "If red touches yellow, it's a dangerous fellow."

The king snake's stripes look almost the same. The king snake is not poisonous, but other animals stay away from it because it looks so much like the coral snake.

king snake

Whose skin is this, covered with fluffy feathers?

This is a snowy owl's skin.

The snowy owl's feathers flutter as it flies, high above the ice and snow. Thick feathers cover the snowy owl's skin— even the skin on its feet. The feathers protect the owl from harsh winter weather.

Fun fact: The male snowy owl is almost pure white. The female snowy owl has gray and black striping. That makes her hard to see in the summer, when she sits in her nest.

Whose skin is this, covered with spots?

This is a caterpillar's skin.

A caterpillar sheds its skin as it grows. Its old skin splits and falls off. A new, bigger skin is uncovered.

Fun fact: When a swallowtail caterpillar first comes out of its egg, it is small, shiny, and black and green. Birds don't try to eat it, because its skin makes it look like a bird dropping.

Each skin has markings on it that protect the caterpillar. Those "eyes" on the front of this spicebush swallowtail caterpillar are really just big, black spots. They fool birds into thinking that it's a snake.

Whose bare skin is this?

This is your skin!

Your skin makes sweat to keep you cool on a hot day. It makes goose bumps when you're cold. It heals cuts, burns, and bruises. It can feel a breeze or the blazing sun. Your skin grows as you grow bigger. What else can your amazing skin do?

Fun fact: Like a caterpillar, you also shed skin, but not all at once. Little pieces of old skin are falling off you all the time. A lot of the dust you see around the house or classroom is actually made up of tiny bits of people's skin.

# Just for Fun

MAKE YOUR OWN FINGERPRINT Look closely at the tiny lines on your fingertips. A good way to get a better look is to make a fingerprint. Just press your fingertip on a stamp pad. Then press your finger onto a piece of paper. No one else in the whole world has fingerprints just like yours.

**MORE FUN WITH FINGERPRINTS—BE A DETECTIVE!** Once you and your friends have copies of your fingerprints, it's easy to play detective. Pretend you need to catch an art thief. Make your own painting and put a stamp pad and wet paper towel near it. Cut enough slips of paper for the number of people playing. Write "art thief" on one slip and "detective" on the rest. Fold up the slips and have everyone pick one. One person will be the art thief, and the rest will be detectives. Don't tell which slip you got.

Next, everyone closes their eyes, except the art thief. All together, count slowly to 20. If you are the art thief, press your finger on the stamp pad and leave a fingerprint on the painting. Be as quiet as you can. When you are done, wipe the ink off your finger with the paper towel.

When the group reaches 20, everyone may open their eyes. Compare the fingerprint on the artwork to each person's fingerprint. Can you figure out who was the art thief?

# Fun Facts About Skin

**QUICK-CHANGE ARTIST** A chameleon has special skin that lets it show different colors. A chameleon can change color depending on the light, the temperature, or even its mood. Sometimes a chameleon's color matches the things around it. A male chameleon might turn a brighter color to warn away other males or to get a female's attention.

**FOOLED YOU!** When the frilled lizard senses danger, it spreads out the loose skin around its neck. The skin fans out and makes the lizard look bigger. If that fails to scare its enemy, the frilled lizard runs to a tree and holds very still. The lizard's body looks like tree bark, making other animals think that it is just part of the tree trunk. Coloring that helps an animal blend in with things around it is called camouflage.

**BOTTOMS UP** The furry skin of a sloth helps it live upside down. Have you ever noticed when you pet a dog that its fur grows down from its back to its belly? The sloth's fur grows the opposite way, from its belly up to its back. The sloth spends most of its life hanging by its claws from tree branches. The sloth's backward fur makes water drip off its belly as it hangs upside down in the wet rain forest.

**PARACHUTE SKIN**  A flying gecko is a lizard with loose fringes of skin on its sides and legs, and between its toes. When the flying gecko feels threatened, it leaps to safety. The skin works like a parachute to keep the gecko gliding as it jumps from one treetop to another.

**RADIATOR RAT**  The naked mole rat doesn't have fur, but it has a neat way to stay warm. It lives in tunnels under the hot desert. When a group of naked mole rats gets cold, one rat makes its way up to a tunnel near the ground's warm surface. Once it gets toasty warm, the rat scurries back to its nest below. The other mole rats cuddle up next to their warm nest mate. They soak up the warm rat's heat through their thin skin.

# Words to Know

**camouflage**  Camouflage is a pattern or color on an animal's skin that makes it blend in with the things around it.

**protect**  To protect is to keep something from being harmed.

**shed**  To shed means to fall off. Some animals shed old skin to make room for new skin.

# To Learn More

## AT THE LIBRARY

Collard, Sneed B. *Animal Dazzlers: The Role of Brilliant Colors in Nature.* New York: Franklin Watts, 1998.

Lauber, Patricia. *Fur, Feathers, and Flippers: How Animals Live Where They Do.* New York: Scholastic, 1994.

Zoehfeld, Kathleen. *What Lives in a Shell?* New York: HarperCollins, 1994.

## ON THE WEB

Lincoln Park Zoo
http://www.lpzoo.com
Explore the animals at the Lincoln Park Zoo.

San Diego Zoo
http://www.sandiegozoo.org
Learn about animals and their habitats.

Want to learn more about animal skin?
Visit FACT HOUND at
http://www.facthound.com

# Index